Understanding Grammatical Names and Functions

Ralph Nyadzi

Published by Cegast Academy, 2024.

While every precaution has been taken in the preparation of this book, the publisher assumes no responsibility for errors or omissions, or for damages resulting from the use of the information contained herein.

UNDERSTANDING GRAMMATICAL NAMES AND FUNCTIONS

First edition. July 12, 2024.

Copyright © 2024 Ralph Nyadzi.

ISBN: 979-8227088444

Written by Ralph Nyadzi.

Also by Ralph Nyadzi

Regrets
The Self-Support Guide
Becoming Self-Employed
Understanding Grammatical Names and Functions
Second Class Citizen Summary & Analysis
The Lion and the Jewel Summary & Analysis
WAEC Literature Poetry: Summary & Analysis
What Makes A Hater
Living to Impress Sucks
Excel in Exam English by Strategy

Watch for more at https://www.cegastacademy.com.

Table of Contents

Understanding Grammatical Names and Functions.....................................1

INTRODUCTION 2

GRAMMATICAL FORM (GRAMMATICAL NAME) – MEANING AND EXAMPLES EXAMPLES...................................4

GRAMMATICAL FUNCTION – MEANING & EXAMPLES .10

STUDY NOTES ON GRAMMATICAL NAMES AND FUNCTIONS (DETAILED EXPLANATION)..............................24

PART ONE: PARTS OF SPEECH (WORD CLASSES) 25

NOUNS...27

VERBS..35

ADJECTIVES 38

ADVERBS 43

PREPOSITIONS 49

PRONOUNS 51

DETERMINERS...53

ARTICLES...56

CONJUNCTIONS..57

EXCLAMATIONS 59

PART TWO: PHRASES..61

THE NOUN PHRASE (NP) 63

THE ADJECTIVE PHRASE/ ADJECTIVAL PHRASE................66

THE ADVERB PHRASE/ ADVERBIAL PHRASE.......................67

THE PREPOSITIONAL PHRASE 69

THE VERB PHRASE 73

PART THREE: CLAUSES 75

THE NOUN CLAUSE (NOMINAL CLAUSE) 76

THE RELATIVE CLAUSE / ADJECTIVAL CLAUSE..................83

THE ADVERBIAL CLAUSE 85

THE VERBLESS CLAUSE..90

100+ GRAMMATICAL NAME AND FUNCTION PAST QUESTIONS AND ANSWERS 92

REVISION EXERCISE: QUESTIONS AND ANSWERS 113

Understanding Grammatical Names and Functions

NEW REVISED EDITION

INTRODUCTION

———

This book, Understanding Grammatical Names and Functions, is a long-awaited response to numerous requests from students and teachers to have a one-stop book on grammatical names and functions. The book addresses most (if not all) of the issues regarding the simple understanding of grammatical names (grammatical forms) and grammatical functions in English.

Now you have it.

Is it the definition of grammatical form or name that you are looking for? Do you wish to learn how to easily identify and state the grammatical name and function of an expression? Maybe you want to have a better understanding of the various parts of speech in English and also can quickly state the part of speech of any word in a sentence.

For some students and teachers of the English Language, having a large collection of examples, questions and answers on grammatical names and functions would be a dream come true.

Well, these and a lot more are what you will find here. At the end of it all, please, do not hesitate to send me a message regarding anything that has to do with this book. I have done everything humanly possible to give you clear and dependable explanations and examples of each topic about how to identify and state the part of speech or grammatical name and function of an expression.

But do not forget. I am still human so I may have committed an error or made a mistake somewhere. Feel free to let me know what you think.

Finally, allow me to give you a word of hope.

There is nothing impossible in this world. What we need to overcome any challenge is to have an open and positive mind, and be determined to do all that we can, never leaving any room for negative thoughts. I have seen thousands of students follow this universal truth to go on and conquer this topic with full marks. It is entirely possible for you too.

I wish you good luck

GRAMMATICAL FORM (GRAMMATICAL NAME) – MEANING AND EXAMPLES EXAMPLES

The terms 'grammatical form' and 'grammatical name' mean the same thing. They are used interchangeably. Remember this all the time as you go through this book on how best to state the grammatical name and function of any expression in a sentence.

The major examples of grammatical forms are word classes such as nouns, verbs, adjectives and adverbs together with their corresponding phrases and clauses. The grammatical form of a given expression in a sentence, therefore, could be anything from a noun or adjective to a noun phrase or adverbial clause.

One important reason for you to study grammatical forms is that you may be asked to state the grammatical form of selected words or groups of words from a sentence. That is if you are a high school or college student who expects to take a test in an English paper.

As a curious independent adult learner interested in learning more about how language functions, knowledge of grammatical forms will be a great addition to your linguistics toolkit.

By the end of this tutorial, you should be in a position to know what is expected from you any time you have to state the grammatical form of an expression in a sentence or a passage.

Additionally, you must know the difference between grammatical form and grammatical function so that you can give the right answer to such

English grammar questions. So I will show you the difference between the two as well.

Definition of Grammatical Form

BEFORE WE IDENTIFY the examples of grammatical forms, I want you to learn the definition of grammatical form. When you know what the term grammatical form re- ally means, you will be in a much better position to answer exam questions on grammatical forms. So here is your simple definition of grammatical form.

Grammatical form is a term used to describe or name a linguistic unit that forms part of a sentence or clause. The particular grammatical form of a linguistic unit is usually based on its composition, structure and function in a sentence.

Remember also that the linguistic unit in question could be a single word or a group of words.

Another term often used to refer to grammatical form is **grammatical name.**

Grammatical Form vs. Grammatical Function

THE BASIC DIFFERENCE between grammatical form and grammatical function is that while grammatical form deals with **the name given to a grammatical unit** made up of a single word or a group of words, a grammatical function has to do with **the role of the grammatical unit** (grammatical form) in relation to other grammatical units within the context of a sentence.

This is why the expressions we use to state a grammatical form's function in a sentence may sound in any of the following ways.

It is the object of the verb .....

Its function is the subject of the verb...

It qualifies the noun ...

Modifier of the verb ...

It is a complement of the preposition...

Examples of Grammatical Forms

EXAMPLES OF GRAMMATICAL forms are nouns, verbs, adjectives, adverbs, pronouns, noun phrases, noun clauses, adjectival phrases and adjectival clauses.

As you can see, grammatical forms fall under word classes [4](also known as parts of speech), phrases and clauses.

We shall now have a few examples to illustrate each type of grammatical form.

Word Classes/Parts of Speech

THE EXAMPLES OF GRAMMATICAL forms that fall under parts of speech (also known as word classes), as we have seen already are nouns, verbs, adjectives, adverbs and so on.

Let's take each example of the grammatical form in this category and illustrate it further with an example.

1. Noun

Example: She has a keen interest in lawn **tennis.**

2. Adjective

Example: She has a **keen** interest in tennis.

3. Verb

Example: As prices **rise**, the value of a currency **depreciates.**

4. Adverb

Example: Hold it **firmly.**

5. Pronoun

Example: **She** spoke fondly about her college years.

6. Determiner

Example: **The** national debt is getting unsustainably high.

7. Preposition

Example: What gifts will you buy **for** Christmas **on**

Amazon?

8. Conjunction

For example, Harvard **and** Yale are prestigious centres of learning.

Phrases

Here are more examples of grammatical forms that are phrases.

9. Noun Phrase

Example: **These same issues** dominated **the discussions** about **the increasing role** of **big tech** in **our global economy.**

10. Adjective Phrase

Example: He wore **very old** shoes to the party.

11. Adverb Phrase

He arrived **too late** for the board meeting.

12. Prepositional Phrase.

Example: I saw a few saloon cars **on the road.**

The following examples of grammatical forms are clauses. Have a look.

13. Noun Clause/Nominal Clause

Example: Tell everybody **that job openings are still available.**

14. Adverbial Clause/Adverb Clause

Example: I didn't receive the email **because my phone had a problem** I couldn't fix immediately.

15. Adjectival Clause/Adjective Clause

McGraw is the programmer **who wants to invent the most powerful antivirus software.**

GRAMMATICAL FUNCTION – MEANING & EXAMPLES

Examples of grammatical functions are subject, object, subject complement, object complement, modifier of a verb, modifier or qualifier of a noun, complement of a preposition, appositive and complement of a verb. In this post, I will give you practical examples of grammatical functions in English to help you understand them better.

The list contains examples of grammatical functions for the most commonly used grammatical names. These are noun/noun phrase/noun clause, adjective/ adjectival phrase/adjectival clause and adverb/ adverbial phrase/adverbial clause.

PLEASE NOTE.

Throughout this tutorial, I will use the below expressions interchangeably.

Adjective phrase/adjectival phrase

Adverb phrase/adverbial phrase

Secondly, nouns, adjectives and adverbs refer to their phrase forms and clauses as well.

Are you ready to have examples of grammatical functions? Then let's get started.

List of Grammatical Functions of Nouns

THERE ARE, AT LEAST, 11 grammatical functions of nouns in English.

Here is the list of all the most common grammatical functions of nouns. Remember that the grammatical functions of nouns are mostly the same for noun phrases and noun clauses as well.

1. Noun Phrase Head

A noun can function as the head of a noun phrase. This means that it is the main word in that group of words and, for that matter, gives the phrase its distinctive name – **Noun** Phrase.

Examples

In each of the following noun phrases, the word in bold lettering is a noun. It functions as the head of the noun phrase.

1. an important **idea**

2. a very difficult **assignment**

3. many **people**

4. the **crux** of the matter

5. my favourite **teacher**

2. Subject

Another function of a noun is the subject of the main verb in a sentence or simply the subject of the sentence. The noun phrase and the noun clause also perform the same function in a sentence.

Examples

In these sentences, the noun/noun phrase/noun clause is in bold lettering. It functions as the subject of the main verb in the sentence.

1. **Food** is expensive these days.

The main verb here is 'is'.

2. **All those men** live near the factory. The main verb is 'live'.

3. **What made us nervous** forced us to abandon the plan.

The main verb here is 'forced'.

4. **Tech companies** hold the key to the prosperity of nations.

The main verb is 'hold'.

5. **Data Science professionals** are in high demand. The main verb is 'are'.

3. Object

A noun/noun phrase/noun clause may function as the object of a verb. It can either be a direct object or an indirect object.

Direct Object Examples

1. It blocks **the road.**

2. No one made **a move.**

3. It brought **many sweeping changes.**

4. I know **the answer.**

5. Who drank **my coffee?**

Indirect Object Examples

1. She sang **the crying baby** a song.

2. Give **those girls** your book.

3. She didn't bring **Michelle** the stolen dresses.

4. Have you given **William** what he asked for last night?

5. I can still sell **them** my new car.

4. Complement

Sometimes, a noun, noun phrase or noun clause functions as the complement of a verb. There are two types of complement here. They are subject complement and object complement.

Next in our list of grammatical functions is 'subject complement'. The subject complement is one of the major functions of nouns.

Subject Complement Examples

See below examples of how a noun functions as a subject complement in an English sentence.

The noun/noun phrase is in bold lettering.

1. John is **my best friend.**

2. Rising prices remain **a major challenge.**

3. Our goal was **total victory.**

4. They were **our only hope.**

5. This is **the child of my brain** and the product of my endeavour.

6. I am **Dickson**, the manager of this hotel.

Object Complement Examples

Just as we have a subject complement, so do we have an object complement. See below examples of object complements in a sentence.

1. Who made you **a judge** over us?

2. I call Akua **my sunshine.**

3. They elected him **captain** of the team.

4. Will the Prime Minister appoint Sunak **Chancellor of the Exchequer?**

5. I can make Francis **my right-hand man.**

5. Prepositional Complement/ Complement of a Preposition

Nouns/Noun phrases/Noun clauses also function as complements of prepositions.

Examples

1. The rise of **social media influencers** is one of the effects of the technological revolution.

2. Digital products will eventually replace much of

what we used to know.

3. TikTok is obviously on **the way** to overtaking well-known tech giants.

4. Have you ever travelled to **the Caribbean?**

5. The celebrations lasted for **several weeks.**

6. I wish I could live in **Port Harcourt.**

7. It depends on **how the players will respond**.

6. Noun Phrase Modifier

In the list of grammatical functions is a noun phrase modifier. Yes, a noun can modify or qualify another noun.

Examples

1. The **New York City** mayor pledged to promote law and order.

2. Sophia Hall is an **investment** banker.

3. To qualify for a **bank manager** job, you need a degree in finance.

4. He is a **software** engineer.

5. The **London** Stock Exchange is one of the busiest in the world.

7. Determinative

A noun can function as a determinative (determiner) in a sentence.

Examples

1. The **pastor's** daughter is a popular YouTuber.

2. You need to follow your **doctor's** advice.

3. This **car's** engine is very new.

4. Tell me your **boyfriend's** story.

5. I will never go to **Mary's** house.

6. **John's** friend is our teacher.

7. They couldn't locate the **baker's** place of work.

8. Adjunct Adverbial

The function of adjunct adverbial forms part of the list of grammatical functions in English grammar.

Quite often, nouns perform the traditional functions of adverbs. They modify verbs and point to the place, time, and so on of an action.

Examples

Take a look at examples of grammatical functions in this category.

1. We will go **home.**

2. I will see you **tomorrow.**

3. Did you arrive **this morning**?

4. She travelled **overseas.**

5. They will come on **Monday afternoon.**

9. Appositive

This is one of the least talked-about examples of grammatical functions. But we use nouns as appositives as often as the other types of grammatical functions.

A noun functions as an appositive (noun in apposition to another noun) when it refers to the same entity the preceding noun refers to.

Examples

1. Anderson, **my friend from Sweden**, is a tech blogger.

2. General Electric, **the American car manufacturer**, produces many other goods.

3. This is my brother Kofi, **the mechanical engineer.**

4. Ezoic, **an AI-powered display ad platform**, is making a lot of publishers rich.

5. They worshipped Zeus, **king of the gods.**

Examples of Grammatical Functions of Adjectives

Our next set of examples of grammatical functions will focus on adjectives.

Typically, adjectives perform the following functions.

- Head of an adjective phrase

- Qualifier/Modifier of a noun/noun phrase

- Subject complement (predicative adjectives)

- Object complement

Here are examples of the grammatical functions of adjectives.

10. Head of an Adjective Phrase

An adjective phrase or adjectival phrase derives its name from the word class or part of speech that the most important word in the group belongs to - adjective.

The adjective functions as the head of the adjective phrase since without it, the group of words would cease to function as an adjective phrase.

Examples

1. Online shopping is *extremely* **popular** in the US and Canada.

2. A *very* **kind** lady gave me this money.

3. Koroma now drives a *completely* **new** car?

4. The cost of starting an online business is *quite*

low.

5. Tricia made a *surprisingly* **funny** remark about the whole affair.

11. Qualifier/Modifier of a Noun/ Noun Phrase

The next example of grammatical functions in English is when an adjective functions as a qualifier or modifier of a noun or noun phrase.

Examples

1. Wise and Paypal are **international** payment platforms.

2. Samsung manufactures smartphones and **desktop** computers.

3. Do you really need a **different** credit card for that purchase?

4. I shop online for my **essential** kitchenware.

5. **Wealthy** people live below their means; poor people don't.

12. Subject Complement

Earlier, we saw this example of a grammatical function with respect to nouns. Adjectives also function in the same manner.

Examples

1. It was **nice.**

2. Your work here is **commendable.**

3. Her income from that online business remains

high.

4. Your certificate seems **genuine.**

5. That insurance company is **reliable.**

13. Object Complement

Quite often, adjectives function as complements of the objects in the sentence.

Examples

1. The incident made her **happy.**

2. You rendered it **worthless.**

3. Does she consider paragliding **risky?**

4. Excessive debt will render you **bankrupt.**

5. The jury found the accused **blameless.**

6. Can you make me **rich**?

Examples of Grammatical Functions of Adverbs

Finally, you are going to see examples of grammatical functions with regard to adverbs.

Adverbs function in the following ways.

· Head of an adverb phrase

· Modifier (intensifier) of an adjective

· Modifier of a verb

· Modifier (intensifier) of another adverb. Let's take them one by one.

Head of an Adverb Phrase

This situation occurs when the group of words is considered an adverbial phrase because the most important word in that group is an adverb. The adverb thus functions as the head of the adverb phrase.

Examples

Very **well**

Quite **slowly**

So **carefully**

Too **kindly**

Rather **stupidly**

Pretty **fast**

15. Modifier of an Adjective

Sometimes, too, an adverb can be seen modifying an adjective.

Examples

Very kind

Well trained

Amazingly beautiful

Too sure

Increasingly popular

Astonishingly frank

Very powerful

Purely absurd

16. Modifier of a Verb

This is arguably the most popular function of adverbs.

1. They left the office **very early**.

2. Digital technology is **rapidly** changing our lives.

3. Solar panels will **soon** cost nothing.

4. Lending rates have fallen **significantly**.

5. Machine Learning courses will **quickly** become the norm.

Examples of Grammatical Functions of Prepositions and Prepositional Phrases

Prepositions

Prepositions help show the relationship between two nouns or objects.

Examples

　　1. Jane sat **on** the chair.

　　2. Malik ran **through** the courtyard.

Also, prepositions tend to introduce nouns in phrases called prepositional phrases.

Examples

On the chair

Through the courtyard

In our school

Near my door

Beyond the sky

With dignity

Under pressure

Between the two parties

17. Qualifier (Modifier) of a Noun

A prepositional phrase can function as an adjective.

Examples

1. A boxer **in the ring** turns into something different.

2. The seat **near my door** was what he wanted.

18. Modifier of a Verb

A Prepositional Phrase can function as an adverb.

1. She cried **with dignity.**

2. Malik ran **through the courtyard.**

19. Complement of an Adjective

A prepositional phrase can serve as the complement of an adjective.

Examples

1. It is obvious you are scared ***of that Rottweiler.***[7]

2. He said he was tired ***of her constant nagging.***

20. Verb Phrase Complement

Prepositional phrases often complement the main verb in a sentence.

Examples

1. I need you to focus **on what is at stake now.**

2. It depends **on several factors.**

3. Would you like to speak **about your problems?**

4. Do not listen **to that guy.**

STUDY NOTES ON GRAMMATICAL NAMES AND FUNCTIONS (DETAILED EXPLANATION)

Carefully go through these study notes to help you better understand grammatical names and functions.

These notes on grammatical names and functions are good for teachers looking for easy-to-follow classroom lesson notes on grammatical names (grammatical forms) and their functions.

Students and independent learners who wish to teach themselves English Language topics such as parts of speech, grammatical names and functions, these study notes will find them extremely useful.

PART ONE: PARTS OF SPEECH (WORD CLASSES)

THE WORD IN A SENTENCE

Consider the sentence:

The whale swallowed Jonah.

It is made up of individual words – four in number (i.e. the. whale, swallowed *and* Jonah)

Every English sentence is like a community of different families.

Look at this analogy:

SENTENCE: Community

WORDS: Individual members from different families

So the sentence above can be said to be a community of different families.

Now just as every individual has a distinctive family name (e.g. Patel, Zelensky, Acquaye, Babangida, Arinze, Tsikata, Brown, Mackenzie, Gosh) so does every word in the sentence have a name. These names are referred to as **parts of speech or word classes.**

You can easily identify every word in a sentence by its family name (part of speech)

The first step to this easy identification is to know these family names (parts of speech) viz.

i. Noun ii) Verb iii) Pronoun iv) Exclamation v)
Adjective

> vi. Adverb vii) Conjunction viii) Preposition ix) Determiner
> / Article

NOUNS

You have to be able to identify a noun when one is underlined in a sentence. So we shall go straight to discover the chief characteristics of words called nouns.

As you might have learnt already, a noun is defined generally as: *"**The name of a person (Dzifa, Peace, Richard, Dela, Kwaku, Glory, Doris, Kafui, Dzigbordi, Patience), thing (table, bulb), quality (kindness, love), place (palace, market)"*** and so on.

So the underlined words in the sentence below are nouns: She put the **book** on the **table**.

However, the above definition alone may not be enough to help you fish out any noun in a sentence. For that matter, we shall presently look at some other important attributes of nouns.

1. Many English words may be called nouns depending on the way they are **used.**

Consider the following sentences:

a. Baaba gave me a beautiful **flower** on Valentine's Day.

b. Trees **flower** in May.

c. There are many **flower** gardens in Norway.

Whereas in sentence (a) **flower** is a noun, it is a verb in (b) and an adjective in (c). "Flower" is **used** differently in different sentences.

2. Many nouns, particularly the so-called common nouns, can be **preceded by a determiner/article or modifier (adjective)**

> Example: the <u>boy</u>; a great <u>day</u>; an <u>unfortunate</u> legacy, an <u>attempt</u>; any <u>idea</u>, Jack Moro's very bitter <u>experience</u>

> Thus any word which is preceded by a determiner/article or modifier is most likely a noun.

> **3.** Many nouns, particularly common nouns have plural forms denoted by the **suffix '-s' or '-es'**

> Examples: activists, rooms, mangoes, shrines, babies, computers.

> Mind you, not all nouns admit the suffix '-s' for their plural forms, though very many do.

4. Nouns often name ...

- Persons e.g. Kofi, Kamala, Jerry, Clinton, Ogata, Zelensky

- Places e.g. Nebraska, Kosovo, East Timor, Oklahoma, Baghdad, Lagos, Takoradi, Freetown, Mumbai, Pretoria, Beirut, Doha, Oakland, Chicago

- Abstractions e.g. love, pride, power, glory, happiness, dignity, confusion.

5. Certain compound words are nouns e.g. Attorney-General, passer-by commander-in-chief, mother-in-law, fire-alarm, life-jacket, sports-wear.

6. Certain words which may not, in their original forms, be regarded as nouns, turn into nouns when they change their form through

affixation. In other words, words **with certain affixes/suffixes tend to be nouns.**

Examples are:

i. 'er' / 'or' – baker, boxer, lecturer, operator, teacher, producer

ii. 'cy' – intimacy, papacy, diplomacy

iii. 'ist' – geologist, activist, communist, herbalist

iv.'ship' – friendship, scholarship, hardship, courtship, dictatorship, relationship

v.'tion' / 'sion' – operation, abortion, corruption, consumption, conclusion, moderation.

vi.'ism' – socialism, racism, neo-colonialism, imperialism

vii.'hood' – childhood, priesthood, brotherhood, parenthood, falsehood.

viii.'ness' – restlessness, bitterness, happiness, greatness faithfulness, togetherness

ix.'ence' /'ance' – excellence, competence, confidence, eminence, insolence, importance, compliance

x.'ment' – government, punishment, enlargement

xi. 'ing' – going, coming, understanding

Note that these 'ing' forms can be **used** as nouns.

Example: When the **going** gets tough, the tough gets going.

It is only when they are **used** that you can say whether they belong to the class of nouns or not.

They are sometimes referred to as 'gerunds' or simply the 'ing – forms'. That is when they are nouns.

xii. 'ty' – modesty, honesty, humility, chastity

You may do well to find out more of these suffixes and add them to the list.

7. Nouns usually refer to:-

i. Physical phenomena Example: earth, sky, moon, shirt, nose, apple, wood, sand, table, (these may be referred to as **concrete nouns**)

8. Certain words, which are constantly in the plural form (pluralia tantrum), are nouns e.g. arms, masses, outskirts, belongings, species, and whereabouts.

9. Certain words which are in apparent plural forms but denote singularity are nouns e.g. Economics, mathematics, physics, classics, linguistics.

10. Certain words formed by joining verbs to prepositions are nouns e.g. pickup, take-off, grownup, offspring.

11. Many nouns have possessive forms e.g. the **king's** crown, the **soldier's** bravery.

12. Some nouns are always used with **'the'** except when they are used with other nouns. e.g.

· The **Kremlin;** Kremlin officials

· The **UK;** UK officials

· The **US;** US officials

· The **Gambia;** Gambian embassy

FUNCTIONS OF A NOUN

1. SUBJECT

A NOUN MAY FUNCTION as the <u>SUBJECT</u> of a verb in a sentence.

Example:

a. <u>William</u> *had* no choice, but in any event he could see no reason to refuse

b. <u>Cracks</u> *appeared* in the curved vault

c. <u>Swimming</u> *is* an enjoyable sport

Please note: The underlined words are nouns.

1. OBJECT (of a transitive verb)

i. <u>DIRECT OBJECT</u> (of a mono-transitive verb

Example:

a. They *made* <u>holes</u> in the curved vault.

b. Jacob *likes* <u>Economics.</u>

c. Mr. Simpson *praised* <u>Affful.</u>

d. ECOWAS member states pledged to *pursue* <u>integration.</u>

e. They *initiated* <u>plans</u> to *curb* <u>desertification.</u>

ii. <u>INDIRECT OBJECT</u> (of a ditransitive verb)

e.g. We *gave* <u>Elias</u> an education instead of riches.

1. COMPLEMENT

SUBJECT COMPLEMENT

The noun which functions as subject complement refers to the same entity the subject refers to. Verbs which produce the subject complement are called LINKING VERBS

Example: **be** (am, are, is, was, were, become, etc), feel, look, stay, remain, turn, cost, come to, consist of, weigh, equal, make etc.

Consider the following sentences.

a. The subject we treated yesterday *was* <u>Linguistics</u>

b. They *remained* <u>friends</u> after that big fight.

OBJECT COMPLEMENT

The noun which is object complement refers to the same thing that the object refers to.

Special verbs produce the object complement. They are called **COMPLEX TRANSITIVE VERBS**. Examples: make, name, crown, call, take, elect, nominate, choose, declare, baptize, and pronounce (these

are also sometimes called **declarative verbs**).

a. The delegates unanimously *elected* Ato

<u>**chairman.**</u>

b. Don't *call* me <u>**manager.**</u>

c. After many weeks of negotiations they will *crown* the most suitable candidate <u>**king.**</u>

d. The Tupac Amaru rebels *took* the Japanese Ambassador **hostage.**

Note that "Ato", "me", "the most suitable candidate" and "the Japanese Ambassador" are the objects in the above examples and the nouns in bold lettering function as object complements.

1. ADJECTIVE/QUALIFIER/MODIFIER

A word, which is traditionally a noun, may perform the function of many adjectives (i.e. qualify an-

other noun)

e.g. a) When we visited the UK last summer my uncle took me to the <u>**London**</u> Bridge.

b. We have a <u>**flower**</u> garden at the back of our house.

c. I found a <u>**blue**</u> pen on the ground

d. Mr. Victor Yankah is a <u>**university**</u> lecturer.

<u>1.</u> APPOSITIVE

e.g. a) My brother, **Dela,** is a pharmacist.

b. Dr. Abbey, <u>**the economist,**</u> addressed the conference.

c. Let the former earl, <u>**Bartholomew**</u>, be told of my decision.

The underlined words are **nouns in apposition** to the nouns/noun phrases before them.

1. COMPLEMENT OF PREPOSITION:

e.g. 1) Doreen travelled by **bus**

2. A large number of **people** decided to listen to her.

3. It is on **record** that more young people are contracting HIV.

4. You are in **trouble.**

VERBS

The Cambridge International Dictionary of English defines a verb as: "a word or phrase that describes an action, condition or experience"

Example: see, hear, dig, run, perform, announce, celebrate, fight

The above definition is a key factor that can help you identify a word as a verb in a sentence.

There are, however, other characteristics of verbs.

1. It is possible to have certain words turned into verbs by attaching certain suffixes or prefixes.

E.g. – ize (Brit) – ise (Aus/ Am) e.g. emphasize, characterize, materialize, sermonize, popularize.

· en – e.g. enjoy, enrol, endear, enlist

· ify e.g. identify, nullify, clarify, codify, signify, quantity, fortify

· ate e.g. incorporate, elongate, substantiate, invalidate

2. A verb normally has a simple past or 'ed' form e.g. came, took, filled

... and a past participle or 'en' form – e.g. drawn, taken, filled, fallen

3. A verb can be a **lexical verb** meaning it can operate on its own without the help of another verb.

e.g. follow, ask, speak, energize

4. On the other hand, it may be an auxiliary verb

There are two main categories of the auxiliary verb:

i. **Primary auxiliary** verbs e.g. do, have, be

ii. **Modal auxiliaries** e.g. can, need, must, ought to, should, dare, would

FUNCTIONS OF THE VERB

a. A verb may introduce the predicate part of a sentence

Example: We **visited London zoo**

THE UNDERLINED PART of the sentence is the predicate and it is introduced by the verb, **visited**

b. The participle or – ing form of the verb may function like an adjective/qualifier.

My mother brought me a **dancing** doll.

c. The past participle or ed/en form of a verb may function like an adjective.

i. All that she got from the fight was a **broken** jaw.

ii. The points presented are **distorted** facts.

d. The participle or -ing form may be used like a noun and therefore perform any of the functions that a noun performs (e.g. objects, subject). Here are two examples for you.

He enjoys **travelling** during summer holidays (object)

Sightseeing is my hobby (subject).

ADJECTIVES

1. The adjective is identified by its characteristic function as a **qualifier of nouns.** Some well-known adjectives are: *good, bad, new, old, beautiful, blue, happy, sure.*

Adjectives often denote physical qualities, such as colour, shape, size, make, and origin; and evaluative quantities like clever, stupid and so on.

1. Quite several adjectives have certain suffixes that help identify them. Some of these are:

-Ic – metallic, tragic, phonetic, basic, academic

-al – medical, controversial, mechanical, biblical, presidential

-some – handsome, troublesome, quarrelsome, fearsome

-ous – generous, conscious, rebellious, dangerous

-ate – unfortunate, compassionate, intemperate

-ful – beautiful, wonderful, fanciful, careful, colourful

-ive – objective, comprehensive, conducive, massive

-ish – foolish, roguish, yellowish

-ble – admirable, unbelievable, uncontrollable, admissible

-ar – lunar, polar, nuclear, familiar

a) Except for a few, adjectives are gradable, In other words, they can be expressed in the comparative form or the superlative form by attaching to them 'er' and 'est' respectively or they can be intensified.

E.g. long longer, longest.

- Some are graded by adding a separate adverb

e.g. attractive, more attractive, most attractive.

- There are few irregular gradable adjectives

e.g. good, better, best

bad, worse, worst

- Gradable adjectives can be intensified by the use of intensifier adverbs such as those underlined below:

· He is <u>so</u> handsome.

· It is <u>rather</u> complicated.

· She is <u>too</u> beautiful.

- The few NON-GRADABLE adjectives include: entire, main, unique, essential, final, round, perfect, eternal, daily

e.g. 'It is unique' BUT NOT 'It is <u>**more/so/very**</u> unique'

FUNCTIONS OF THE ADJECTIVE

1. Basically, adjectives specify, qualify, or modify nouns in noun phrases. (While some adjectives can come only before

the noun, some can operate only after the noun. But some can operate either before or after the noun or after the verb)

a. An adjective that qualifies a noun by coming before the noun is said to be a **PRE-MODIFIER** (i.e. It pre-modifies the noun)

Examples:

i. A <u>medical</u> student

ii. A <u>beautiful</u> day

iii. <u>Absolute</u> nonsense (absolute here is an intensifier adjective)

iv. The <u>same</u> day

v.A <u>complete</u> fool (complete here is also an intensifier adjective)

vi. The <u>current</u> crisis

vii. A <u>young</u> doctor

viii. The <u>famous</u> writer

b. An adjective that qualifies a noun by coming after the noun is said to be a **POST- MODIFIER** (i.e. It post modifiers the noun)

Examples:

I. SOMETHING <u>good</u>

ii. God <u>Almighty</u>

iii) Joyful Way <u>Incorporated</u>

iii. Generations <u>unborn</u>

iv. President-elect

c. An adjective which qualifies a noun by appearing after the verb is said to be a **predicative adjective**. (i.e. It qualifies/ modifies the noun by appearing in the predicate part of the sentence.)

e.g. i) She is <u>asleep.</u>

ii. Kofi is <u>afraid.</u>

iii. I am <u>fine.</u>

iv. The patient appears <u>strong</u>

v. He was <u>drunk</u>

vi. The girl is <u>beautiful</u>

vii. We are <u>ashamed</u> to speak about our weaknesses.

2. Certain adjectives function as heads of noun phrases

Examples:

i. The <u>wretched</u> of the earth

ii. The <u>weak</u>

iii. The <u>powerful</u>

iv. The <u>poor</u>

v. The <u>rich</u>

vi. The <u>downtrodden</u>

vii. The <u>chosen</u>

viii. The <u>privileged</u>

Note that the underlined words are adjectives (not nouns). They are only functioning like nouns (as heads of noun phrases). Phrases of this kind are also called **quasi-noun phrases.**

3. Certain adjectives do not just qualify but are intensifiers placed before nouns.

Examples:

<u>absolute</u> certainty

<u>complete</u> disaster

<u>deep</u> concern

<u>great</u> importance

<u>high</u> proportion/quality

<u>perfect</u> happiness/timing

<u>profound</u> silence/implications

<u>strong</u> support

<u>stiff</u> opposition

<u>tremendous</u> amount/pressure/opportunity

<u>utter</u> rubbish/ confusion.

ADVERBS

A. One way to identify an adverb in a sentence is provided by the definition given in the Cambridge International Dictionary of English.

An adverb is a word which describes or gives more information about a verb, adjective, adverb or phrase.

In the following sentences, cheerfully, spotlessly, extremely, well and right are adverbs.

i. She smiled <u>cheerfully</u>

ii. The house was <u>spotlessly</u> clean.

iii. He is managing <u>extremely</u> well.

iv. The shot was heard <u>right</u> outside the door.

b. Another characteristic of adverbs is that they usually have the affix '-ly' attached to them. Most of these are derived from adjectives. e.g. fortunate – fortunately

Others include: shortly, briefly, importantly, mostly, normally,

c. A few adverbs begin with the morpheme 'a-'

e.g. abroad, ahead, abreast, around, aloof, alert, astray

d. A few adverbs have the suffixes – 'like', '- wise', '-ward'

Examples:

He walked <u>crablike.</u>

Note, however, that **crablike** is an adjective in:

This is a <u>crablike</u> behaviour.

e. Some adverbs have comparative and superlative forms.

e.g. – well, better, best

· Little, less, least

· Far, farther/further, farthest

· Badly, worse, worst

· Much, more, most

· Soon, sooner, soonest

f. A large number of adverbs take the same form as adjectives. Such words are only identifiable as adverbs (or adjectives) depending on the function they perform in a sentence.

Example:

i. Frankie Fredericks ran very <u>fast</u> (adverb)

ii. Frankie Fredericks is a <u>fast</u> runner (adjective)

Others are *quick, hard, daily, late, long, early, round, high, only, far, past.*

g. Many adverbs take the form of **conjunctions.** These words often introduce subordinate/dependent clauses and are, therefore, sometimes referred to as **subordinating conjunctions.** We shall look at them when we discuss clauses.

e.g. when, why, though

i. Tell me <u>when</u> to stop

ii. I don't know <u>why</u> Charlotte fought her twin brother.

h. 'This' can be used as an adverb (meaning 'as much')

Example:

She has never been <u>this</u> late for school.

FUNCTIONS OF AN ADVERB

1. An adverb may function as an **adjunct providing more information about the verb** in terms of how, where, when or how often (something happens).

A. HOW? (ADJUNCT OF Manner)

· We enjoyed the film <u>greatly</u>.

· Daddy Lumba sings <u>beautifully</u>.

b. Where: (Adjunct of Place)

· Let's go <u>inside</u>

· The people who live <u>upstairs</u> are very noisy.

Note, however, that in the sentence,

Sadly, the <u>upstairs</u> of the office building was gutted by

fire, <u>upstairs</u> is a noun performing the function of a **subject**

c. When? (Adjunct of Time)

· I haven't read the newspaper <u>yet</u>

· It is going to rain <u>soon</u>

d. How often? (Adjunct of Frequency)

· We <u>never</u> ate fufu on Sundays.

· Priscilla <u>seldom</u> visits us.

· I will <u>always</u> remember Nana Esi.

1. Adverbs also function as **disjuncts.** In other words, adverbs provide information about the speaker's or writer's viewpoint or attitude.

· <u>Surprisingly</u>, all the children came on time.

· <u>Politically</u>, that was a bad decision.

· <u>Clearly</u>, Lizzie is a serious student.

1. Adverbs function as **conjuncts** (i.e. they join two clauses, sentences, or paragraphs together).

Words like, first, next etc. could be conjuncts (or adjectives) depending on how they are **used in a particular sentence.**

Other conjuncts can be seen in the following examples.

i) I talked to him <u>then</u> I pleaded with him <u>so</u> he changed his mind.

i. She has been to jail on several occasions <u>yet</u> she refuses to change her ways.

1. The adverb functions as a **modifier/intensifier** of a verb, an adjective or an adverb or a prepositional phrase. Most of these adverbs are adjuncts of manner.

a. Intensifier of a verb

· The car <u>almost</u> crashed.

· The medicine helped him <u>enormously</u>.

· He <u>just</u> did it.

· Sackey was discharged after he had <u>fully</u> recovered.

b. Modifier/intensifier of an adjective

e.g. i) it is <u>very</u> unfortunate

Note, however, that "<u>very</u>" becomes an adjective (meaning EXACT) when it is used in such sentences as:

Sandra is the <u>very</u> woman I will marry.

ii. The Clinton administration was <u>enormously</u> popular both in America and in the rest of the world.

c. Modifier/intensifier of another adverb/adverbial phrase

e.g. i) We will finish <u>quite</u> soon.

ii) Akofa speaks <u>amazingly</u> fast.

ii) It happened all <u>too</u> soon.

d. Modifier/intensifier of a prepositional phrase.

· The glass broke <u>right</u> down the middle.

PREPOSITIONS

A. The Cambridge Dictionary defines a preposition as **"A word which is used before a noun, a noun phrase or a pronoun, connecting it to another word"**

The underlined words in the sentences below are prepositions.

· We jumped <u>into</u> the lake

· She drove slowly <u>down</u> the track

Technically, therefore, the preposition is that word which **expresses a relationship between two entities; be they objects, actions or movements.**

b. Some common propositions are: in, on, of, off, at, after, before, into, onto, for, with, to, under, behind, below, beneath etc. These are **simple prepositions**

c. <u>COMPLEX PREPOSITIONS</u>

i. Adverb/preposition + preposition: e.g. He stood <u>away from</u> the crowd.

ii. Verb/adjectives/conjunction + proposition e.g. because of, depend on, responsible for

iii. Preposition + Noun + Preposition: e.g. by dint of, under the auspices of

FUNCTIONS OF THE PREPOSITION

A. A PREPOSITION EXPRESSES a relationship between two entities (objects actions, etc) in terms of:

i. Place:

The boy is standing **under** the tree (i.e. it expresses the relationship between <u>the boy</u> and <u>the tree</u> in terms of place)

ii. Time:

The examination will take place **on** Monday

iii. Instrument:

He stabbed the murderer **with** a dagger.

iv. Accompaniment:

He walked in the garden **with** his mistress.

v. Reason/purpose:

They killed him **for** money

b. A preposition introduces a prepositional phrase.

e.g. He met her **behind** the house.

c. A preposition may function as an adverb.

E.g. Stay **off** the game reserved. (Place)

Get **inside** the car. (Place)

PRONOUNS

---

a. A pronoun is a word, which is used instead of a noun, a noun phrase or a nominal group. Pronouns are often used to refer to nouns that have already been mentioned.

E.g.

i. Tom bought <u>himself</u> a radio

ii. 'Let's go out tonight' <u>That's</u> a good idea'

iii. The eggs were cheap so we bought <u>twelve</u>. ('Twelve' is used here pronominally. That is to say, like a pronoun)

b. Pronouns take different forms:

e.g. Some, none, few, many, any, something, nothing, everything, everyone, everybody, anything, anybody, anyone, this, that, these, those, one, one's, one another, each, each other,

The more common pronouns include:

I, me, mine, myself, we, us, ours, ourselves, he, him, his, himself, hers, she, her, herself, it, itself, they, them, theirs, themselves, you, your, yourself, yourselves, who, who, which, whichever, whoever, what, whatever.

Note that such words as *my, our, your, their, its, her,* and *his are not considered pronouns but rather* DETERMINERS

FUNCTIONS OF THE PRONOUN

a. A pronoun may replace/refer to a noun or a whole statement that has just been mentioned or is about to be mentioned.

e.g. I know Tim Walz very well. <u>He</u> is an honest person. <u>That</u> I know.

<u>He</u> refers to 'Tim Walz' and <u>that</u> refers to 'He is an honest person'.

b. <u>SUBJECT:</u>

A pronoun just like a noun may function as the subject of a sentence.

e.g. a) <u>I</u> saw the boy

b. <u>They</u> met President Harris in the White House.

c. <u>OBJECT:</u>

e.g. We caught <u>him</u> at Sakora Park

DETERMINERS

Determiners are used before nouns or noun phrases to make clear which particular person or thing is meant or to give information about quantity.

e.g. <u>The</u> government, <u>a</u> brush, <u>some</u> water, <u>five</u> oranges, the <u>other</u> leg, <u>your</u> eyes.

A few determiners can be used **before other determiners.** They are thus called PRE-DETERMINERS

e.g. **<u>both</u>** these apples, **<u>all</u>** that time, **<u>half</u>** the money, **<u>twice</u>** the profit.

Adjectives can come between the determiner and a noun e.g. <u>her</u> *new* dress.

NOTE:

1. Some words are used as both determiners and pronouns

a. They are called determiners when they appear before a noun.

e.g. **any** news, **few** people, **which** car.

b. They are pronouns when they are used alone, to replace a noun. e.g.

· There isn't **<u>any</u>**.

· Only a **<u>few</u>** turned up

· She didn't tell me **<u>which</u>**.

2. Numbers may be used as:

a. <u>Determiners (before a noun)</u>

e.g. There were **seven** actors on stage.

b. <u>Pronouns (replacing a noun)</u> e.g. The actors came on stage in groups. There were **seven** at first.

c. <u>As nouns:</u>

e.g. Two **seven** is fourteen

DIFFERENT FORMS OF DETERMINERS

I. MY, HER, HIS, ITS, our, your, their,

These are also referred to as **possessive determiners**

ii. This, these, that, those, (they are sometimes called **demonstrative pronouns/adjectives**)

iii. What, which, whose, (They are also called **relative pronouns.** This is when they are **used** as pronouns)

iv. Whichever, whatever

v. Either, neither

vi. Other, another

vii. Every, all each, both, some, any, many, most, much, lots of, few, several, a little, enough, no (these refer to quantity)

viii. The (also called definite article)

ix.A/An (also called indefinite article)

FUNCTIONS OF THE DETERMINER

I. THEY ARE USED TO modify/qualify nouns and noun phrases (just like adjectives) in terms of:

a. Specifying a particular person or thing e,g. <u>That</u> picture looks funny.

b. Giving information about quantity

e.g. <u>All</u> my money has been stolen.

Words like ***all, twice, both*** etc are also called **predeterminers.**

ARTICLES

Articles are mostly used before nouns to refer to people, ideas and so on. Thus, articles are determiners; the only difference being that only a few determiners are articles.

EXAMPLES

I. **The** (also sometimes referred to as "definite article")

ii. **A, an** (also sometimes referred to as indefinite articles)

FUNCTIONS OF ARTICLES

I. AS DETERMINERS, articles qualify nouns and noun phrases (Please, refer to FUNCTIONS OF DETERMINERS (i) a)

ii. Articles qualify adjectives e.g.

a. The young are idealistic.

b. The French love fashion.

c. The government is unpopular among the unemployed.

d. She was the first to finish.

e. China was the fastest-growing economy in Asia.

CONJUNCTIONS

A. Conjunctions are words that connect units of language namely words, phrases and clauses

b. <u>FORM:</u>

1. ***But, and, or.*** These are simple coordinators

2. Correlative Conjunctions

· Both ... and,

· Not only ... but

· Neither ... nor

· Either ... or

· Whether ... or

3. Quasi Coordinators

· As well as

· Together with

· Along with etc

4. Subordinating Conjunctions.

Unless, as, if, because, since, though etc.

FUNCTIONS OF CONJUNCTIONS

A. A CONJUNCTION MAY join two words together

e.g. i) Joyce <u>and</u> Ralph were once great friends.

ii) I like it <u>whether</u> cold <u>or</u> hot

b. A conjunction may join two phrases together.

e.g. i) I admire <u>both</u> the bold <u>and</u> the beautiful.

ii) All the students <u>as well as</u> their headmaster were involved in the scandal.

c. A conjunction may join two clauses (main clause and subordinate clause) together. It is those conjunctions which per- form this function that are called subordinating conjunctions. In other words, they introduce the subordinate clause.

EXAMPLES

1. a) <u>As</u> he could not find the smugglers, he decided to cross the border.

b) He decided to cross the border <u>as</u> he could not find the smugglers

2. a) He would have passed the examination <u>if</u> he had studied harder.

b) <u>If</u> he had studied harder he would have passed the examination.

EXCLAMATIONS

Exclamations are used to show strong feelings of anger, surprise, disgust etc. They are also used to greet someone, make a request or to agree to something.

Note that exclamations are usually used in informal communication.

FORM: Exclamations do not normally change their grammatical form:

i. Wow (surprise)

ii. Damn (anger)

iii. Ugh (disgust)

iv. Hi, hello (greeting)

v. Please (request)

vi. Okay (agreement etc)

vii. Phew (disgust)

viii. Hurray (joy, triumph)

Note that the exclamation is not limited to the interpretations found in brackets here. In fact, the particular situation and speaker's tone could suggest a different attitude, feeling or emotion.

An exclamation mark '!' (Which is essentially a punctuation mark) is used, usually immediately after the exclamation.

FUNCTIONS OF EXCLAMATIONS

THEY SEEM TO PERFORM more literary functions than strictly grammatical functions.

Thus the exclamation may help to show the speaker's attitude, state of emotion etc. These may be related to joy, anger, pain, surprise, disgust, etc.

As already stated, the context (situation) within which a particular exclamation occurs goes a long way in determining its possible interpretations.

PART TWO: PHRASES

———

Two helpful definitions of a phrase are:

i. A group of words that has no finite verb, no subject and no predicate.

ii. A group of words of which one is the head (the most important word) with the others in the group modifying or qualifying it (the head).

Indeed, a single word may be considered a phrase without a modifier. Thus, a phrase may be represented mathematically as:

[Modifier/Qualifier] + Head + [Modifier /Qualifier]

The implications of the above representation include the following:

i. A phrase may include a premodifier/premodifiers

ii. A phrase may include a post modifier/post modifiers

iii. A phrase must of necessity include a head word.

Note that <u>the part of speech</u> of this head word gives the phrase its name e.g. <u>noun</u> phrase, <u>adjective</u> phrase etc.

NB: i) 'Pre' and Post' are terms used in the description of modifications within the noun phrase.

ii) **A prepositional phrase** is a special phrase which does not conform to the above formula and its implications. We shall explain this further at the appropriate time.

The other types of phrases, apart from the prepositional phrase, are:

i. Noun phrase

ii. Adjective phrase

iii. Verb phrase

iv. Adverb phrase

THE NOUN PHRASE (NP)

The noun phrase could be represented as:

[Determiner(s)/Premodifier (s)] + Head + [Post modifier(s)]

The 'Head' here should obviously be a **noun**. Examples:

A noun phrase can be as simple as:

a. The <u>scientist</u>

b. A large <u>association</u> of traders

c. All our <u>children</u>

d. An old <u>tree</u>

e. <u>Candle</u> in the wind

f. The <u>girls</u>

Again, a noun phrase can be as complex as:

a. The <u>scientists</u> who secretly met President Harris concerning the falling asteroid.

b. An extremely large <u>association</u> of angry traders in the Makola market who were ordered out of the pavements by the Accra Metropolitan Assembly

NB: The head words of the above noun phrase are underlined. It must be noted that within the rather long and complex noun phrases in (b) above, there are other phrases and even clauses. Can you find these out?

FUNCTIONS OF THE NOUN PHRASE

NOUN PHRASES FUNCTION the same way nouns do.

i. <u>SUBJECT OF A VERB</u>:

e.g. <u>The civil war</u> **dragged** on into the New Year.

ii. <u>OBJECT OF A VERB</u>:

e.g. Philip **had** <u>only a few seconds</u> to decide whether to repudiate <u>the whole deal</u>.

iii. <u>COMPLEMENT</u>

a. SUBJECT COMPLEMENT:

e.g. It **was** <u>an odd thing to do</u>.

b. OBJECT COMPLEMENT

e.g. The legal system in the Caribbean has long ago **made** the British Privy Council <u>the final court of appeal</u> particularly in cases involving capital punishment.

iv. <u>COMPLEMENT OF A PREPOSITION</u>

e.g. He felt that the air **of** <u>bustling efficiency</u> did him credit. The preposition, as you can see, is **of**

v. <u>APPOSITIVE</u>

e.g. Philip, <u>the prior of Kingsbridge,</u> has arrived.

vi. <u>ADJECTIVE / QUALIFIER</u>

A phrase, which is essentially a noun phrase, may perform the function of an adjective. In other words, a noun phrase may function as a qualifier of another noun phrase.

e.g. <u>a highway</u> **casual labourer**

The underlined noun phrase is qualifying another noun phrase, <u>casual labourer</u>

THE ADJECTIVE PHRASE/ ADJECTIVAL PHRASE

The adjective phrase could be represented as: (Intensifier adverb) + Head.

The 'head' should obviously be an **adjective.**

Example: a) Very <u>poor</u>.

b. So <u>good</u>

c. Amazingly <u>beautiful</u>

d. Potentially <u>bloody</u>

e. Too <u>true</u>

f) Purely <u>governmental</u>

FUNCTIONS OF THE ADJECTIVE PHRASE

QUALIFIER OF A NOUN/ NOUN PHRASE:

e.g. The UN failed to foresee a <u>potentially bloody</u> **civil war** in Rwanda

e.g. The <u>new digital</u> **system** technically known as "Next 61" has a higher speed of transmission.

THE ADVERB PHRASE/ ADVERBIAL PHRASE

The adverb phrase could be represented as:

(Intensifier Adverb) + Head (With the 'head' being the main adverb).

Examples:

a) Marvelously <u>well</u>

b. Very <u>shortly</u>

c. Quite <u>often</u>

d. Rather <u>sadly</u>

e. So <u>fast</u>

f) Pretty soon

FUNCTIONS OF THE ADVERB PHRASE

THE ADVERB PHRASE MAY function as an **adjunct or disjunct modifying a verb.**

a. <u>ADJUNCT</u>

i. Adjunct of manner (how?)

e.g. The secretary general's speech was <u>very well</u> **delivered.**

ii. Adjunct of place (where?)

e.g. "**Move** <u>right across</u> the mine field", the soldier ordered the P. O. W.s

    iii. Adjunct of time (when?)

e.g. The delegation will **arrive** <u>pretty soon</u>

    b. <u>**DISJUNCT**</u> (providing information about the speaker's or writer's viewpoint or attitude)

e.g. Christie's gone away for nearly six months but <u>strangely enough,</u> Ralph, her boyfriend, **cares** little about it.

THE PREPOSITIONAL PHRASE

THE STRUCTURE OF THE PREPOSITIONAL PHRASE

The prepositional phrase may be represented as any of the following:

i. Propositon + Noun phrase

e.g. a) in the church

b. of government revenue

c. in a business

d. to the product

e. for the promotion

f. of a staff member

g. at one time

ii. Preposition + Wh – Clause

e.g. a) from where he stood

b. for what he believed in

c. to where she lodged her complaint

d. on whatever you say

iii. Preposition + - ing form / clause

e.g. a) with singing the same song

b. at dancing

c. by running fast

d. on manufacturing toys

iv. Preposition + Adverb

e.g. a) before long

b. at once

c. at least

v. Preposition + Prepositional phrase

e.g. a) from under the table

b. from below the bridge

FUNCTIONS OF THE PREPOSITIONAL PHRASE

1. **ADVERBIAL** (i.e. It functions like an adverb modifying the verb element in the sentence.)

A. ADJUNCT:

e.g. i) **I met** him <u>at the party</u> (adjunct of place modifying the verb 'met')

ii. She **wept** <u>in the darkness</u> (adjunct of place modifying the verb "wept")

iii. They **exchanged** gifts <u>during the festivities</u> (an adjunct of time modifying the verb "exchanged")

iii) He **spoke** <u>with authority</u> (an adjunct of manner modifying the verb "spoke")

b. Conjunct:

e.g. i) <u>On the contrary,</u> they **gave** me little help.

ii. <u>In the first place,</u> I **wish** you a Happy New Year.

iii. <u>In brief/in a nutshell</u> the policy **was** a disaster.

c. Disjunct

e.g. i) <u>To my surprise,</u> Adjoa **passed** the English test.

ii) <u>In fact,</u> you've **disappointed** us

2. ADJECTIVAL (POST – MODIFIER OF A NOUN PHRASE)

e.g. i) Cegast is **a centre** <u>of academic excellence.</u>

ii. Neil Armstrong undertook **a journey** <u>to the moon</u>

iii. No one can deny the fact the Chief Nanga was **a man** <u>of the people.</u>

Can you identify the noun phrases that the prepositional phrases are post – modifying? They are (i) a centre (ii) a journey and (iii) a man.

3. COMPLEMENT OF A VERB

e.g. (i) The S.O.S Village **looks** <u>after orphaned children</u>.

(ii) It all **depends** <u>on a lot of factors</u> Identify the verbs the prepositional phrases are complementing.

4. COMPLEMENT OF AN ADJECTIVE

e.g. (i) He is **afraid** <u>of beautiful ladies</u>.

ii. I am **tired** <u>of waiting</u>.

iii. They said they were **sorry** <u>for their wayward sister</u>.

THE VERB PHRASE

The verb phrase may be represented as: (Auxiliary Verb) + Main Verb + (Adverb)

e.g. (i) Has arrived

ii. Will provide

iii. Could have gone

iv. Started slowly

An adverb may appear within a verb phrase. One example is (iv) above. Here is another one:

could have <u>easily</u> won.

FUNCTION OF THE VERB PHRASE

THE VERB PHRASE FUNCTIONS as the predicator in a sentence. In other words, **it introduces the predicate part** of a sentence or clause.

e.g. Graphic Corporation <u>has been formally incorporated</u> as a limited liability company under a new name, Graphic Communications Group Limited.

Note that the subject part of the sentence is:

Graphic Corporation

and the predicate part is:

has been formally incorporated as a limited li- ability company under a new name, Graphic Com- munications Group Limited.

PART THREE: CLAUSES

A clause is a group of words made up of a subject and a verb (finite or non–finite).

One practical difference between a clause and a phrase is that a clause looks and sounds more like a sentence than a phrase.

A clause, therefore, sounds more meaningful than a phrase.

For that matter, it is easier to directly pick a complete sentence from most clauses than from phrases. This is usually the case where the clause is a finite clause.

Example:

1. Melody knew <u>that her sister was not in the room</u>.

Since we can pick a complete sentence (i.e.***her sister was not in the room*** from this underlined group of words, we can say that it is a clause.

2. Hamza knew <u>that man's character</u>.

Since there is no way we can directly pick a complete sentence from the underlined group of words, we can say that it is a phrase.

THE NOUN CLAUSE (NOMINAL CLAUSE)

B efore we look at their functions, let us first identify the various structural forms of the noun clause (nominal clause).

1. NOMINAL RELATIVE CLAUSE

THOUGH THIS TYPE OF clause looks like a relative clause, it is not one. Rather, it is a nominal (noun) clause.

In other words, it does not qualify anything but rather behaves like a noun.

A nominal relative clause is usually introduced by a

wh-word.

e.g. a) <u>What Ralph is looking for</u> is a meaningful

life.

b) I want to see <u>whoever deals with complaints</u>

<u>here</u>.

   c. We shall uncover <u>who did it</u>.

d. You are free to vote for <u>whichever candidate you like</u>.

e. Home is <u>where your friends and family are</u>.

2. NOMINAL TO – INFINITIVE CLAUSE

IT IS SO CALLED BECAUSE (i) It has a non – finite verb element

(ii) It is introduced by 'to'

e.g. a) My ambition is <u>to be an influential author and publisher</u>.

b. <u>To err</u> is human.

3. NOMINAL "BARE INFINITIVE" CLAUSE

In this clause, the 'to – element' is absent but implied. It usually makes use of the verb 'do'.

e.g. All I **did** was <u>turn off the gas.</u>

NOTE THAT 'TO' COULD have conveniently come before 'turn'

Other examples are:

a. The only thing she could **do** was <u>cry</u>.

b. All that he **did** was <u>hit him hard twice</u>.

4. NOMINAL – 'ING INFINITIVE' CLAUSE

i. This is a non – finite clause

ii. It is introduced by an – ing participle.

e.g. a) Some people enjoy <u>deceiving their friends.</u>

b. Benyiwah's hobby is <u>collecting stamps</u>

c. <u>Being treated like a fool</u> is what I hate.

5. THE NOMINAL "THAT' – CLAUSE

AS THE NAME IMPLIES, this type of clause is usually introduced by the word 'that'.

However, you must note that "**that**" may also be used to introduce a relative clause. One way to help you see the difference is to take note of the pronunciation of 'that' which is barely stressed in the case of the **noun clause.**

Try saying: She thinks **that I will be there.**

It goes up (with greater emphasis) in the case of the **relative clause/ adjectival clause.**

Try saying: The girl **that showed up** was not the one I was looking for.

Also, where **that** introduces a noun clause, it is impossible to replace **that** with **who, whom** or **which.**

This will become clearer as we look at the function of the relative clause.

e.g. The farmers have realized <u>that locust invasions are seasonal</u>.

Sometimes, however, the **'that'** is omitted and is only implied. Even in this case the clause is a nominal that – clause, or better still, a **zero nominal that – clause.**

    e.g. I can see <u>you are busy</u>

'that' is omitted but implied in between 'see' and 'you'.

    e.g. I can see <u>(that) you are busy</u>.

6. NOMINAL WH – INTERROGATIVE CLAUSE

THIS NOUN CLAUSE TYPE seeks to **ask a question** and is introduced by such wh – words as **where, when, which, what,** and **why.** ('How' is also included).

e.g. a) <u>Why he did it</u> is beyond my imagination.

b. <u>How the books will sell</u> depends greatly on its cover.

c. I can't imagine <u>what made him behave rudely</u> toward the King.

d. Nobody knows <u>what is wrong with this world</u>.

7. NOMINAL "YES/NO INTERROGATIVE" CLAUSE

THIS TYPE OF NOUN CLAUSE (nominal clause) is derived from a question that demands a yes or no answer.

It is usually introduced by 'if' or 'whether'

e.g. a) <u>Whether I will attend the party</u> depends on certain factors.

b. I don't know <u>if the banks will remain open during the holiday.</u>

c. <u>Whether I can play or not</u> does not concern the minister.

FUNCTIONS OF THE NOUN CLAUSE

AS IT BEHAVES LIKE a noun, the noun clause or nominal clause performs all the functions that a noun may perform.

It must however be made clear that while some individual types of the nominal clause (noun clause) seem to perform all the functions of a noun, some others perform only some of these functions.

The nominal clause may function as:

1. <u>SUBJECT OF A VERB</u>

Example:

a. <u>That Bedie was ousted</u> did not **surprise**

most political observers.

b. <u>What he has in store for us</u> may never

come to be.

c. <u>To forgive</u> **is** divine.

d. <u>Change my mind</u> **is** all I can do.

2. <u>OBJECT OF A VERB:</u>

i. <u>Direct object</u>

Example:

a. I **told** him <u>that he was wrong</u>.

b. Everybody **knows** <u>that the economy is in distress</u>

c. Can you **guess** <u>if he will turn up?</u>

d. He **hates** <u>obeying instructions</u>.

ii. <u>Indirect object:</u>

Example:

a. She **offered** <u>whoever visited her</u> soft drinks.

b. My dog **gives** <u>whatever it sees in the night</u> a searching look.

c. They **gave** <u>swimming in the crocodile pond</u> a serious appraisal.

<u>3. COMPLEMENT:</u>

i. <u>SUBJECT COMPLEMENT</u>

Example:

a. This **is** <u>what we've been looking for</u>

b. The truth **is** <u>that you cannot always run away from justice</u>.

ii. <u>OBJECT COMPLEMENT:</u>

Example:

a. They **made** her <u>what she should be.</u>

<u>4. COMPLEMENT OF AN ADJECTIVE</u>

Example:

a. Researchers are **certain** <u>that a cure will be found for the AIDS disease eventually</u>.

b. I am so **glad** <u>that Jesus loves me.</u>

c. He is **difficult** <u>to convince.</u>

d. The children were **busy** <u>building sandcastles</u>.

f. William was **curious** <u>to see it more close- ly</u>.

<u>5. COMPLEMENT OF A PREPOSITION</u>

Example:

a. It depends **on** <u>how you look at it.</u>

b. The refugees slept **on** <u>what they could find</u>.

c. I am interested **in** <u>finding a solution to the problem</u>.

<u>6. APPOSITIVE</u>

Example:

a. His **ambition**, <u>to be the president of the local NUGS</u>, was never realized.

b. Your **question**, <u>whether I will accept the bribe</u>, is not necessary

c. The **day**, <u>when Christ will return</u>, is unknown.

d. Your **assertion**, <u>that ghosts are real</u>, may not be accepted by some Christians.

THE RELATIVE CLAUSE / ADJECTIVAL CLAUSE

The relative clause is often introduced by a relative pronoun – **who, which, whose, that**

Note that "**that**" as a relative pronoun introducing a relative clause can easily be replaced by **which** or **who** or **whom** with the construction still making sense.

Try replacing 'that' in a nominal that – clause (noun clause introduced by 'that') with **who, whom** or **which** and you will see that it makes no sense.

Examples of relative clauses:

a. The boy <u>who is standing there</u> is my friend.

b. The man <u>whose food I ate</u> will soon arrive.

c. The cat <u>that ate my fish</u> stole my meat too.

It is significant to note that sometimes the relative pronoun may be omitted but is implied. In that event, the clause remains a relative clause or better still, a zero relative clause.

e.g. Some ladies <u>I met yesterday</u> claimed they were American tourists.

You can see that a relative pronoun (whom/who) is implied between 'ladies' and 'I'

i.e. Some ladies <u>(whom) I met yesterday claimed they were American tourists</u>.

FUNCTION OF THE RELATIVE CLAUSE/ ADJECTIVAL CLAUSE

<u>POST – MODIFIER IN A NOUN PHRASE</u>

This is the basic function of the relative clause. It is due to this qualifying role in the noun phrase that some people refer to the relative clause as **ADJECTIVAL CLAUSE** (i.e. it behaves/functions like an adjective).

Note, however, that the name <u>RELATIVE CLAUSE</u> is based on the fact that the clause is usually introduced by a <u>RELATIVE PRONOUN</u>.

Let us look at how it functions as a post – modifier in a noun phrase. Example:

I will never forget the man <u>who rescued me from the lion's paws</u>.

Here, the noun phrase is: "The man who rescued me from the lion's paws" and **<u>who rescued me from the lion's paws</u>** is a relative clause qualifying/post–modifying **"the man"**

You can go back to the Section on Noun Phrases if you are a bit confused.

THE ADVERBIAL CLAUSE

A key attribute of adverbial clauses is that they are introduced by certain types of words.

Some of these are: **after, before, until, since, if, though, while, wherever, should, even if, as,** etc.

The non – finite '-ing' and 'ed' forms may also be used in adverbial clauses.

Since there are many types of adverbial clauses, let us try and identify the commonest ones.

1. Adverbial clause of Time:

Words introducing the adverbial clause of time include:

After, before, when, while, whenever, since, until. Examples:

a) The students were seated <u>before the lecturer arrived</u>.

b. <u>Whenever prices of petroleum products go up</u> traders increase the prices of their goods.

c. <u>After seeing you</u>, I realized it was worth the effort

Sometimes the subordinating conjunction may be omitted but implied.

e.g. <u>Going to school</u>, I met a pretty lady.

In this instance, **while, when, while I was,** and **when I was,** are possible beginnings to the clause but are omitted.

e.g. (**While** I was) going to school, I met a pretty lady.

2. Adverbial Clause of Place

Subordinating conjunctions: where, wherever, everywhere etc.

He hit him <u>where it hurt most</u>.

3. Adverbial Clause of Condition

Subordinating conjunctions: If, should, in case, unless, provided)

Example:

a. <u>If we must die</u>, let us not die like hogs.

b. She wouldn't have escaped <u>if she had been put in an iron cage</u>.

4. Adverbial Clause of Concession (There is an element of contrast in it but the idea expressed is not unusual)

Subordinating conjunctions: though, although, while, whereas, even if, whether – or not, no matter, whatever -, however

Example:

a. <u>Though Joshua passed the test</u>, he was not promoted.

b. <u>Whereas Uju seems a clever girl</u> I still need to test her.

c. <u>Even if you turn over a new leaf</u>, I will no longer trust you.

d. <u>Whether living in London or not</u>, Sackey enjoyed himself.

Note that where 'even if' is used, there is very little difference between a clause of condition and a clause of concession, if any at all.

Other examples:

a. <u>Sneer unkindly though you may</u>, Biden is very popular.

b. <u>Naked though I was</u>, I braved the storm.

c. <u>No matter how hard I try</u>, I will never catch up with him.

5. Adverbial Clause of Comparison.

Subordinating conjunctions: as, as-so, less-than, faster-than

Example:

a. <u>As</u> he thinks <u>so he acts</u>.

b. My daughter reacts to situations <u>as I do</u>.

c. Mike walks <u>faster than he runs</u>.

6. Adverbial Clause of Reason

Subordinating conjunctions:

Because, since, as, so -—that, so, in view of, now that, considering the fact that, seeing that.

Example

a. He failed the interview <u>because he took too much for granted</u>.

b. <u>Since you abandoned the children</u> you have no right to claim they are yours.

c. We decided to stop the match <u>as it began to rain</u>.

7. Adverbial Clause of Proportion / Degree

Subordinating conjunctions:

As + as; (the + comparative) + (the + comparative)

Example:

a. As I approached the hill <u>so did the trees loom large before me</u>.

b. <u>The harder</u> we tackle the problem <u>the more difficult it becomes.</u>

8. Adverbial Clause of Purpose

Subordinating conjunctions:

In order (to, that); to, so as to, for fear; so that, etc.

Example:

a. We closed early <u>in order to watch the match live on TV.</u>

b. The baby cried louder <u>so as to draw attention to itself.</u>

9. Adverbial Clause of Manner

In many cases, there is little difference between the clause of manner and that of comparison.

Subordinating conjunctions:

As; as if; as though; (just) as if; as – so Example:

a. Brother Jero behaves <u>as if he's an angel</u>.

b. <u>Just as a goat will bleat when being sent to the slaughter so</u> did he cry on his way to the gallows.

c. He played <u>just as the coach taught him</u>. (i.e. the way the coach taught him to play)

<u>10. Adverbial Clause of Preference</u>

Subordinating conjunctions:

Rather than, sooner than

Example:

<u>Rather than vote for any dishonest candidate</u> I will not vote at all.

FUNCTIONS OF THE ADVERBIAL CLAUSE

THE ADVERBIAL CLAUSE **modifies the verb element in the sentence** by functioning as an adjunct/disjunct of place, time, manner, condition etc.

e.g. He **hit** him <u>where it hurt most</u>.

The underlined adverbial clause functions as an adjunct of place modifying the verb, "hit"

Refer to the examples we have seen so far to avoid repetition.

THE VERBLESS CLAUSE

As the name implies, the verbless clause contains no verb element.

However, the verb (usually "to be") is implied. Note that the verb "to be" consists of **is, are, am, become, was, were, became** and may include others like **appear** and **seem.**

The verbless clause may however contain an infinitive clause (with a non – finite verb)

Examples:

a. <u>Although occasionally unhappy</u> Hannah sings a lot.

b. <u>Helpless,</u> I gave up.

We can again render this as

<u>As I became helpless,</u> I gave up.

FUNCTIONS OF THE VERBLESS CLAUSE

THE VERBLESS CLAUSE very often appears in the domain of adverbial clauses. So it may function in the following ways.

a. <u>Adjunct of Time (i.e. Adverbial Clause of Time)</u>

e.g. i) <u>Once in London,</u> I **started** looking for a job.

You will show your mastery of clauses if you Name the Underlined – **Once in London** – as

<u>verbless adverbial clause</u>

And state its FUNCTION as:

***Adjunct of time** modifying the verb "started"*

    ii. <u>While here</u>, let's discuss the problem.

iii. They said they would address the issue <u>whenever appropriate</u>

    b. <u>Place</u>:

e.g. We will maintain the venue <u>wherever acceptable</u>

    c. <u>Condition</u>:

<u>If really common</u>, we too will get some of it.

    d. <u>Reason</u>:

e.g. <u>Confused</u>, she stood still.

Note: It must be made clear here that the verbless clause is just one (in fact, the third) aspect of the categorization of clauses into

i. Finite clauses

ii. Non – finite (infinitive) clauses and of course

iii. Verbless clauses.

100+ GRAMMATICAL NAME AND FUNCTION PAST QUESTIONS AND ANSWERS

The questions and answers on grammatical names and functions in this section will show you how to provide the most suitable answers in this segment of your English Language test paper.

We are going to provide grammatical name and function answers to each one of the items according to the following type of question that WAEC repeats almost every year.

Do not worry if you're a student or teacher from a different jurisdiction. You can still benefit from this practical demonstration if you are required to answer similar questions in your specific type of English Language test.

The question is in two parts.

·What grammatical name is given to this expression as it is used in the passage?

·What is its function? Or State its function.

DEFINITION OF GRAMMATICAL NAME

AT THE BEGINNING OF this book, we looked at the definitions of grammatical name/grammatical form and grammatical function.

All the same, I will give you another way to define these terms. You will realize that though the wording may differ slightly, the meaning remains the same.

Below is a working definition of the term, "grammatical name".

A grammatical name is the name given to a word or group of words depending on its function and structure in a given clause or sentence.

Whenever it is a single word, your WASSCE (or whichever English Language exam you are facing) question typically asks you to state the PART OF SPEECH of the word in question.

It is usually underlined in the comprehension passage. In this case, you will have to state if the underlined word is a **noun, verb, adjective, adverb, conjunction, pronoun or preposition.**

On the other hand, where it is a group of words, the regular WASSCE comprehension question here is expected to ask for the GRAMMATICAL NAME for the expression.

Over here too, you will have to be able to perform two separate tasks to get your answer correct.

First, you must ascertain whether the group of words is a PHRASE or a CLAUSE.

Secondly, you must be clear in your mind if that phrase or clause is **adjectival, adverbial or nominal/ noun** in its function.

DEFINITION OF GRAMMATICAL FUNCTION

Grammatical function refers to the syntactic role a word or group of words is performing within a given clause or sentence.

PLEASE NOTE THAT WITHOUT any reference to the sentence (the context), you will find it difficult (if not impossible) to identify both the grammatical name and function of a word or expression.

Thus, grammatical function is all about the **behaviour** of a word or group of words **in relation to others** in a given clause or sentence.

What I'm saying is this: Avoid the habit of taking the underlined word or group of words in isolation and then struggling to get what its grammatical name and/ or function are/is.

Please note that the part of each sentence in bold lettering is what we are interested in.

PAST QUESTIONS AND ANSWERS

TEASER GRAMMATICAL NAME AND FUNCTION QUESTION:

· What is the grammatical name of *'legal profession'* in the sentence, *The **legal profession** ranks among the most respected professions in Nigeria.*?

· State its function.

SOLUTION:

Grammatical Name: Noun Phrase

Function: It is the subject of the verb, 'ranks'.

You can now have multiple examples of grammatical name and function questions.

1. **When they talked or swore**, their minds showed a bright pink. NOVEMBER 2014.

Grammatical Name (GN): Adverbial Clause of Time

Function (F): It is modifying the verb, "showed".

2. **Not long after the government's official proclamation** newspaper reporters had a field day. JUNE 2015.

GN: Adverbial Phrase

F: It is modifying the verb, "had".

3. They needed to buy saucepans and pieces of cloth to prepare for marriage **when they returned home**. JUNE 2013.

GN: Adverbial Clause

F: It is modifying the verb, "prepare".

4. People **who speak the same language** feel related to one another. NOVEMBER 2009.

GN: Adjectival Clause

F: It is qualifying the noun, "people".

5. Here he was, inviting contributions on an issue

that was not on the agenda. NOVEMBER 2009.

GN: Adjectival Clause

F: It is qualifying the noun phrase, "an issue".

6. In the waiting room, he met other applicants for the interview, **which had been slated for 9:00 am**. NOVEMBER 2015.

GN: Adjectival Clause/Non-defining Relative Clause

7. In Niger, for example, **the absence of wetlands** has forced the men to break new ground with a fish farming technique which is proving very successful. NOVEMBER 2005.

GN: Noun Phrase

F: It is the subject of the verb phrase, "has forced" (or the verb, "forced").

8. **What you put in your mouth** can change your mood, alertness, memory and clarity of thought. NO- VEMBER 1999.

GN: Noun Clause

F: It is the subject of the verb phrase, "can change" (or the verb, "change")

9. But you have made **a sad mistake** and must suffer the consequences. NOVEMBER 1999.

GN: Noun Phrase

F: It is the object of the verb phrase, "have made" (or the verb, "made")

10. Akua was already **there**, desperately hurling through a window whatever she thought could be salvaged from the pool she stood in. PART OF SPEECH JULY 2003.

GN: Adverb

F: It is modifying the verb, "was".

11. **Although the child's parents are his earliest and most important models**, he is exposed to many other potent influences: siblings, television, school, celebrities and so on. JUNE 2008.

GN: Adverbial Clause (of concession)

F: It is modifying the verb phrase, "is exposed" .(or the verb, "exposed")

12. This reminded me of another father **I came across many years ago**. JUNE 2008.

GN: Adjectival Clause (or Zero Relative Clause: Note that the relative pronoun, WHOM/WHO, introducing this clause is omitted. It should have come just after "father" and before "I")

F: It is qualifying the noun phrase, "another father" (or noun, "father").

13. He was not a hard-hearted man who would cherish **denying a man in distress a favour** but the deplorable condition his car was in made him behave that way. JULY 2004.

GN: Noun Clause

F: It is the object of the verb, "cherish" (or verb phrase, "would cherish")

14. Perhaps no other historical figure exhibited this leadership characteristic better than Richard the Lionheart, the twelfth-century English King, who always led his army **personally into battles**, always maintaining the front position. NOVEMBER 1998.

GN: Adverbial Phrase

F: It is modifying the verb, "led".

15. I only steeled myself for the rebuke from Mr. Nyamekye **who never countenanced ill-prepared papers** such as the one I had written. NOVEMBER 1998.

GN: Adjectival Clause

F: It is qualifying the noun, Mr. Nyamekye.

16. **The community centre** was brimful of expectant citizens when the chief came in. NOVEMBER 2002.

GN: Noun Phrase

F: It is the subject of the verb "was".

17. As she had done on previous occasions, she got out, stood by her car, and donned her **poor-defenceless-woman** look. PART OF SPEECH. GCE JUNE 1997.

GN: Adjective

F: It is qualifying the noun, "look". (Note that the word, "look" as used in the above sentence is a noun and not a verb.)

18. Then she turned round to the elders and chuckled in spite of herself and her **smarting** face. GRAM- MATICAL NAME. YES. GCE JUNE 1997.

GN: Adjective

F: It is qualifying the noun, "face".

19. There was an unknown woman, Madame Legros, **who ran a small tailoring shop,** in France during the French Revolution. NOVEMBER 2001.

GN: Adjectival Clause (or Non-defining relative clause)

F: It is qualifying the noun, "Madame Legros".

20. In addition to this false sense of well-being, the poor **who eventually find their way up the financial ladder** do not read enough to utilize the health information available in the media and other sources of information to help them adopt a healthier lifestyle. NOVEMBER 2001.

GN: Adjectival Clause

F: It is qualifying the noun phrase, "the poor".

21. Although some people like talking about the "good old days", few are ready to give up the many **time-and-labour-saving** devices that they have come to take for granted. GRAMMATICAL NAME GCE JUNE 1996.

GN: Adjective

F: It is qualifying the noun, "devices".

22. Here, the truth is that a victim can tolerate the person who actively inflicts an injury on him quite readily, but finds it much more difficult to forgive the bystander **who** encourages that offender to carry on inflicting his misdeed. GRAMMATICAL NAME AND FUNCTION, GCE JUNE 1998.

GN: Relative Pronoun

F: It is introducing the adjectival clause (or relative clause) "who encourages that offender"

23. Apart from his two new cassocks, Father John owned **hardly anything to write home about.** GRAMMATICAL NAME AND FUNCTION, GCE JUNE 1998.

GN: Noun Phrase

F: It is the object of the verb, "owned".

24. Yet, it is the only organ **that never really rests.**

JUNE 2013.

GN: Adjectival Clause

F: It is qualifying the noun, "organ" (or the noun phrase, "the only organ").

25. It was in that room that I met, for the first time, the commander **who was to me an independent ally.**

GN. Adjectival Clause

F. It is qualifying the noun, "commander".

26. He pronounced **a curse against moving his bones.**

GN. Noun Phrase

F. It is the object of the verb, "pronounced"

27. They heard **a brief strange noise** from the room behind them.

GN. Noun Phrase

F. It is the object of the verb, "heard".

28. I've already asked her to show them **where it is weighed.**

GN. Noun Clause

F. It is the object of the verb, "show".

29. Kindly place it **where it is weighed.**

GN. Adverbial Clause (of place)

F. It is modifying the verb, "place".

30. **The affluent of past decades** would marvel at the sheer volumes of money today's rich people have.

GN. Noun Phrase

F. It is the subject of the verb, "marvel" (or of the verb phrase, "would marvel").

31. She sidestepped **the less important ideas.**

GN. Noun Phrase

F. It is the object of the verb, "sidestepped".

32. **Those little children in the house** need our care and attention.

GN. Noun Phrase

F. It is the subject of the verb, "need". (In other words, it is the subject of the sentence)

33. **The regulation of the earth's temperature** remains one key function of the oceans.

GN. Noun Phrase

F. It is the subject of the verb, "remains".

34. That definitely is **a threat to our environment.** GN. Noun Phrase

F. It is a complement to the verb, "is"

35. **Using words to express ideas** was not a recent development in the history of human communication.

GN. Noun Clause

F. It is the subject of the verb, "was"

36. **Before I could recover from the shock**, she landed a second blow on the other side of my face.

GN. Adverbial Clause (of time)

F. It is modifying the verb, "landed".

37. We would sit there, watching the men **who had come to beg for favours.**

GN. Adjectival Clause

F. It is qualifying the noun, "men".

38. Foreigners **who speak the same language**

bond together quite easily. GN. Adjectival Clause

F. It is qualifying the noun, "foreigners"

39. We never thought **that he would agree to run the state.**

GN. Noun Clause

F. It is the object of the verb, "thought".

40. It is becoming increasingly clear that **if care is not taken,** something terrible may happen before she leaves office.

GN. Adverbial Clause (of condition)

F. It is modifying the verb, "happen". (or the verb phrase, "may happen")

41. **If my mother had had more money** she would have assisted me.

GN. Adverbial Clause (of Condition)

F. It is modifying the verb, "assisted" (or the verb phrase, "would have assisted")

42. **If you read** you would pass.

GN. Adverbial Clause (of condition)

F. It is modifying the verb, "pass".

43. It was **the most devastating moment for the entire troop.**

GN. Noun Phrase

F. It is the complement of the verb, "was".

44. **If society could be understood at all** it would happen in later years.

GN. Adverbial Clause of Condition

F. It is modifying the verb, "happen" (or the verb phrase, "would happen").

45. It raised **an instant alarm**. GN. Noun Phrase

F. It is the object of the verb, "raised".

46. The materials last for ages **when they are used properly.**

GN. Adverbial Clause

F. It is modifying the verb, "last".

47. **Using words to express ideas** is a primary function of language.

GN. Noun Clause (ing-infinitive nominal clause)

F. It is the subject of the verb, "is". (or subject of the sentence).

48. They finally agreed to send him to the native doctor **who alone knew how to cure lunatics.**

GN. Adjectival Clause

F. It is qualifying the noun phrase, "native doctor".

49. **This** disease will soon disappear like a miracle. GN/Part of Speech: Adjective

F. It is qualifying the noun, "disease".

50. **Most human beings** use at least one and some- times two or more languages.

GN. Noun Phrase

F. It is the subject of the verb, "use".

51. **The two hands** rested gently on the child's head.

GN. Noun Phrase

F. It is the subject of the verb, "rested".

52. **If he is lucky** nothing happens to him. Grammatical Name: Adverbial Clause (of Condition)

Function: It modifies the verb, "happens"

53. You begin to lose appetite **because you automatically feel too full.**

Grammatical Name. Adverbial Clause (of Reason) Function: It modifies the verb, "begin".

54. They would have escaped easily **had a stray dog not given them away.**

Grammatical Name: Adverbial Clause (of Condition)

Function: It is modifying the verb, "escaped" (or verb phrase, "would have escaped")

55. Anyone **that had come in contact with the patient** went into quarantine.

Grammatical Name: Adjectival Clause Function: It qualifies the pronoun, "anyone".

56. She was a witness **that had no say in the matter.**

Grammatical Name: Adjectival Clause Function: It is qualifying the noun, "witness".

57. All they could get from him were **inaudible and evasive answers.**

Grammatical Name: Noun Phrase

Function: It is the complement of the verb, "were".

58. The plumber **whose young wife was pregnant with their first baby** came forward.

Grammatical Name: Adjectival Clause

Function: It is qualifying the noun, "plumber".

59. **Since the beginning of this century,** this relative equilibrium of Nigeria's agricultural societies has been disturbed.

Grammatical Name: Adverbial Clause (of Time)

Function: It is modifying the verb, "disturbed" (or the verb phrase, "has been disturbed").

60. **If social man is to be understood at all** we must start by questioning the theories about the origin of the human species.

Grammatical Name: Adverbial Clause (of Condition)

Function: It is modifying the verb, "start" (or the verb phrase, "must start")

61. Any health worker **that had come into contact with the patient** was not spared.

Grammatical Name: Adjectival Clause Function: It is qualifying the noun, "worker".

62. **Four years after the incident**, she continued to blame herself for it.

Grammatical Name: Adverbial Phrase

Function: It modifies the verb, "continued".

63. **An interesting feature of this all** is that nothing is allowed to stand in its way.

Grammatical Name: Noun Phrase Function: It is the subject of the verb, "is".

64. The whole community concluded **that I was missing.**

Grammatical Name: Noun Clause

Function: It is the object of the verb, "concluded".

65. They told us **why they abandoned the idea**. Grammatical Name: Noun Clause

Function: It is the object of the verb, "told".

66. Her ambition was **to be inducted into the Hall of Fame.**

Grammatical Name: Noun Clause

Function: It is the complement of the verb, "was".

67. I would like to know **how WAEC set their questions.**

Grammatical Name: Noun Clause Function: It is the object of the verb, "know".

68. The good news is **you're at liberty to do as you please.**

Grammatical Name: Noun Clause

Function: It is the complement of the verb, "is".

68. I mistakenly thought **she was mine.**

Grammatical Name: Noun Clause

Function: It is the object of the verb, "thought".

69. Salaries **paid to workers** have been woefully in- adequate.

Grammatical Name: Adjectival Clause Function: It is qualifying the noun, "salaries".

70. **In the past few months** I've suffered a lot. Grammatical Name: Adverbial Phrase (of Time)

Function: It is modifying the verve, "suffered" (or the verb phrase, "have suffered")

71. **These days** mark the beginning of her professional blogging career.

Grammatical Name: Noun Phrase

Function: It is the subject of the verb, "mark".

72. That baby hardly sleeps **these days.**

Grammatical Name: Adverbial Phrase (of Time)

Function: It modifies the verb, "sleeps".

73. People **on the road** seem to care very little about the rest of us.

Grammatical Name: Adjectival Phrase Function: It is qualifying the noun, "people".

74. She **then** realized how ignorant she had been all along.

Part of Speech: Adverb (of Time)

Function: It is modifying the verb, "realized".

75. The goldsmith left it **there** for you. Part of Speech: Adverb (of Place) Function: It is modifying the verb, "left".

76. That was a blatant **lie.**

Part of Speech: Noun

Function: It is the complement of the verb, "was".

77. The atmosphere **that now prevails** on the cam- pus is not conducive for academic work.

Grammatical Name: Adjectival Clause Function: It is qualifying the noun, "atmosphere".

78. **This** is all your making.

Part of Speech: Pronoun

Function: It is the subject of the verb, "is".

79. She knows **too well** that she could have done better.

Grammatical Name: Adverbial Phrase (of Manner)

Function: It modifies the verb, "knows".

80. The one **who has cheated** will not escape punishment.

Grammatical Name: Adjectival Clause Function: It is qualifying the pronoun, "one".

81. That dog believes **barking** can get it out of trouble.

Part of Speech: Noun (Gerund/Verbal Noun)

Function: It is the subject of the verb, "get" (or verb phrase, "can get").

81. A **barking** partner is the greatest enemy of any peaceful relationship.

Part of Speech: Adjective

Function: It is qualifying the noun, "partner".

82. Tell me **whose cake is the best.**

Grammatical Name: Noun Clause

Function: It is the object of the verb, "tell".

88. The contestant **whose cake is the best** will receive a cash reward from the organizers.

> Grammatical Name: Adjectival Clause Function: It is qualifying the noun, "contestant".

89. **The end of the road** was not what we thought it would be.

> Grammatical Name: Noun Phrase Function: It is the subject of the verb, "was".

90. **Doing this** will take you nowhere.

Grammatical Name: Noun Clause ("-ing infinitive nominal clause" - For higher level students of grammar)

Function: It is the subject of the verb, "take" (or verb phrase, "will take").

91. They simply gave him **the lifeline of another man.**

> Grammatical Name: Noun Phrase Function: It is the object of the verb, "gave".

92. **Manoeuvring a tanker** poses many challenges.

Grammatical Name: Noun Clause (Non-finite Nominal ing-clause/ Gerund Clause)

Function: It is the subject of the verb, 'poses'.

93. **This situation arises if the head sees himself as a boss.**

Grammatical Name: Adverbial Clause (of Condition)

Function: It is modifying the verb, 'arises'.

94. The lorry **we caught** was old and slow.

Grammatical Name: Adjectival Clause (Note that 'that' or 'which' has been omitted at the beginning of the clause. The sentence should have read, 'The lorry **that/which we caught** was old and slow'.)

Function: It is qualifying the noun, 'lorry'.

95. These concerns **which emerged in the mid-western region of Nigeria** have largely remained unresolved.

Grammatical Name: Adjectival Clause Function: It is qualifying the noun, 'concerns'.

96. They remained **on that mountain** for weeks. Grammatical Name: Adverbial Phrase

Function: It is modifying the verb 'remained'.

97. **When she got down** it was already dark. Grammatical Name: Adverbial Clause Function: It is modifying the verb 'got'.

98. The culprits **who could not pay the fine imposed on them** begged for clemency.

Grammatical Name: Adjectival Clause Function: It is qualifying the noun 'culprits'.

99. **Before leaving my office** the visitors issued a stern warning.

Grammatical Name: Adverbial Phrase (of Time) Function: It is modifying the verb 'issued'.

100. The cattle do not attack the birds **because they feel a special affection for them.**

Grammatical Name: Adverbial Clause (of Reason)
Function: It is modifying the verb 'attack'.

101. The condition **that now prevails** leaves many households poorer.

Grammatical Name: Adjectival Clause Function: It qualifies
the noun 'condition'.

102. **A candidate in an examination hall** normally does everything
possible to perform well.

Grammatical Name: Noun Phrase Function: It is the subject of the
verb 'does'.

*Source: The West African Examinations Council Past Question Papers,
Google and others.*

REVISION EXERCISE: QUESTIONS AND ANSWERS

State the part of speech [POS] or grammatical name [GN] and grammatical function [GF] of each of the underlined words or groups of words in the following sentences.

1. Nelson Mandela made this speech <u>on the day of his release</u> from prison.

2. <u>Our match to freedom</u> is irreversible.

3. President de Klerk announced <u>that apartheid would no longer operate</u>.

4. He appointed Thabo Mbeki <u>as his successor</u>.

5. It is an ideal <u>which I hope to live for and to achieve</u>.

6. You turn <u>if you want to</u>. The lady's not for turning.

7. Margaret Hilda Thatcher was born <u>in London</u> in 1925.

8. She became <u>the Member of Parliament</u> for Finchley in 1959.

9. She was known for her <u>single – minded</u> pursuit of polices which became an increasingly hard-line.

10. But we want a <u>free</u> economy.

11. We believe <u>that you become a responsible citizen</u> by making decisions for yourself.

12. What then stands <u>in our way</u>?

13. I don't like <u>to go and see something that leaves me depressed</u>.

14. I don't like to go and see something <u>that leaves me depressed</u>.

15. <u>After he had driven an ambulance in the First World War</u>, he started animating his drawings.

16. He planned and built Disneyland <u>a huge amusement park</u>.

17. This part <u>eventually</u> opened in 1971.

18. <u>This</u> was how Walt Disney described his early life.

19. Now, <u>when Mickey Mouse came along</u> he made quite a splash.

20. It was necessary for me to give up the drawing <u>in order to organize and run the organization</u>.

21. The kind of films I make I do them <u>because I like to make them.</u>

22. I do <u>them</u>.

23. I just wouldn't feel <u>right</u> trying to do some of these things.

24. I have to fight them <u>sometimes</u>.

25. He made his first <u>animated</u> film.

26. He started <u>running the organization</u>.

27. <u>As I became more accomplished at mountaineering</u>, my ambition became stronger.

28. I wanted <u>to climb harder and harder things</u>.

29. <u>Although he was a beekeeper by profession</u>, he grew increasingly interested in mountaineering.

30. He joined a <u>New Zealand</u> party to the central Himalayas in 1950.

31. In 1953 he made the first <u>successful</u> attempt to climb Mount Everest.

32. Sir Edmund Hillary took part in <u>numerous other expeditions</u>.

33. He became fascinated by mountains <u>when he was a teenager</u>.

34. I learnt <u>to ski</u>.

35. I learnt to ski in a <u>pretty</u> rough fashion.

36. I really enjoyed <u>that</u> enormously.

37. <u>My ambitions</u> became stronger and stronger.

38. He remained <u>very modest</u>.

39. I have always regarded myself as a <u>mediocre</u> individual.

40. I have no <u>particularly remarkable</u> talents.

41. I'm not <u>a great intellectual</u>.

42. An announcer <u>from the BBC</u> was at the top of the mountain.

43. The team were aware of the <u>dangerous</u> conditions.

44. The American Government took away his <u>boxing</u> license for three and a half years.

45. I want the world to know <u>I'm so great</u>.

46. I'm the greatest thing <u>that ever lived</u>.

47. Ali was <u>confident</u> about defending the world heavyweight championship title.

48. <u>While Bill Gates was still in school</u>, he developed a program for arranging a school time table.

49. He describes <u>how he first got interested in computers</u>.

50. My school had a <u>dial-up</u> connection to a computer.

RECOMMENDED ANSWERS TO REVISION EXERCISE QUESTIONS

<u>PLEASE NOTE</u>

GN: **Grammatical Name**

POS: **Part of Speech**

GF: **Grammatical Function.**

1. **GN**: Preposition phrase.

GF: Adverbial of time modifying the verb,

made

2. **GN**: Noun phrase

GF: The subject of the verb, **is**

3. **GN:** Noun clause

GF: Object of the verb **announced**

4. **GN**: Noun phrase

GF: Object complement of the verb, **appointed**

5. **GN**: Relative / Adjectival clause

GF: It is qualifying the noun, **ideal**

6. **GN:** Adverbial clause of condition

GF: It is modifying the verb, **turn**

7. **GN:** Prepositional phrase

GF: Adjunct / Adverbial of place modify- ing the verb, **born**

8. **GN:** Noun phrase

GF: Subject complement of the verb, **be- came**

9. POS: Adjective

GF: It is qualifying the noun, **pursuit**

10. POS: Adjective

GF: It is qualifying the noun, **economy**

11. **GN:** Noun clause

GF: Object of the verb, **believe**

12. **GN:** Prepositional phrase

GF: Adjunct [Adverbial} of time modifying the verb **stands**

13. **GN:** Noun clause (nominal to – infinitive clause)

GF: Object of the verb **like**

14. **GN:** Adjectival clause (or relative clause)

GF: It qualifies the pronoun, **something**

15. **GN:** Adverbial clause of time

GF: It is modifying the verb, **stated**

16. **GN:** Noun phrase

GF: Noun in opposition to the noun, **Dis- neyland**

17. **POS**: Adverb

GF: It is modifying the verb, **opened**

18. **POS**: Pronoun

GF: The subject of the verb, **was**

19. **GN:** Adverbial clause of time

GF: It is modifying the verb, **came**

20. **GN:** Adverbial clause of purpose

GF: It is modifying the verb, **was**

21. **GN:** Adverbial clause of reason

GF: It is modifying the verb, **do**

22. **POS:** Pronoun

GF: Object of the verb, **do**

23. **POS:** Adverb of manner

GF: It is modifying the verb, **feel**

24. **POS:** Adverb of frequency

GF: It is modifying the verb, **fight**

25. **POS:** Adjective

GF: It is qualifying the noun, **film**

26. **GN:** Noun clause [nominal ing – infinitive clause]

GF: Object of the verb, **started**

27. **GN**: Adverbial clause of proportion

GF: It is modifying the verb, **became**

28. **GN**: Noun Clause

GF: It is the object of the verb **wanted.**

29. **GN**: Adverbial clause of the concession

GF: It is modifying the verb, **grew**

30. **POS**: Adjective

GF: It is qualifying the noun, **party**

31. **POS**: Adjective

GF: It is qualifying the noun, **attempt**

32. **GN**: Noun phrase

GF: It is a complement to the preposition,

in

33. **GN**: Adverbial clause of time

GF: It is modifying the verb, **became**

34. **GN**: Noun clause (nominal to-infinitive clause)

GF: Object of the verb, **learnt**

35. **POS**: Adverb

GF: It is modifying the adjective, **rough**

36. **POS:** Pronoun (demonstrative pronoun)

GF: Object of the verb, **employed**

37. **GN:** Noun phrase

GF: The subject of the verb, **became**

38. **GN:** Adjectival phrase (Predicative Adjectival phrase)

GF: It is qualifying the pronoun, **he**

39. **POS:** Adjective

GF: It is qualifying the noun, **individual**

40. **GN:** Adjectival phrase

GF: It is qualifying the noun, **talents**

41. **GN:** Noun phrase

GF: Complement of the verb, **am**

42. **GN:** Prepositional phrase

GF: It functions as an adjective qualifying the noun, **announcer**

43. **POS:** Adjective

GF: It is qualifying the noun, **condition**

44. **POS:** Adjective

GF: it is qualifying the noun, **license**

45. **GN:** Noun clause [zero nominal that – clause]

GF: Object of the verb, **know**

46. **GN:** Adjectival clause [or relative clause]

GF: It is qualifying the noun, **thing**

47. **POS**: Adjective [predicative adjective]

GF It is qualifying the noun, **Ali**

48. **GN:** Adverbial clause of time

GF: It is modifying the verb, **developed**

49. **GN:** Noun clause

GF: The object of the verb, **describes**

50. **POS**: Adjective

GF: It is qualifying the noun, **connection.**

<u>PLEASE NOTE</u>

GN: is **Grammatical Name**

POS: is **Part of Speech**

GF: is **Grammatical Function.**

THE END

Don't miss out!

Visit the website below and you can sign up to receive emails whenever Ralph Nyadzi publishes a new book. There's no charge and no obligation.

https://books2read.com/r/B-A-OQZF-SYXEC

BOOKS2READ

Connecting independent readers to independent writers.

Did you love *Understanding Grammatical Names and Functions*? Then you should read *Excel in Exam English by Strategy*[1] by Ralph Nyadzi!

[2]

Unlock your full potential with **Excel in Exam English by Strategy**, the ultimate revision textbook tailored for high school exit exam candidates. Designed specifically for WAEC/WASSCE candidates, this comprehensive guide equips you with essential strategies to master essay writing, reading comprehension, and summary writing. It's also a pathway to academic achievement for any student preparing for similar examinations.

Inside, you'll find key study guides, a collection of past exam questions, and practical demonstrations that illustrate the best approaches to answering English questions effectively. Whether you're a senior high school student, a teacher seeking valuable resources for

---

1. https://books2read.com/u/b5g816

2. https://books2read.com/u/b5g816

your class, or a parent aiming to support your child's success, this book offers the tools and insights you need to excel.

Here is a golden opportunity for you to join the ranks of successful candidates who have transformed their exam performance with this indispensable guide.

Read more at https://www.cegastacademy.com.

Also by Ralph Nyadzi

About the Author

Ralph Nyadzi founded *Cegast Academy,* a lifelong learning and publishing outfit, in 2001. He teaches English for Academic Purposes (EAP) online and blogs on *bloggingtothemax.com.* Besides teaching part-time and writing full-time, he enjoys cooking and staying close to nature. Ralph lives in southern Ghana.

Read more at https://www.cegastacademy.com.

About the Publisher

Cegast Academy is the sole publisher of books authored by Ralph Nyadzi and other authors who are happy to work with him.
Read more at https://www.cegastacademy.com/.